MW00877811

12TH AND FINAL SIGN OF THE ZODIAC
FEBRUARY 19 TO MARCH 20

PISCES TRAITS:

EMPATHETIC

SENSITIVE

PSYCHIC

ADAPTABLE

DREAMY

GENEROUS

CURIOUS

CREATIVE

NAIVE

GULLIBLE

Made in the USA
Columbia, SC
19 December 2022

74606838R00057